CREEPY BUT COOL
CATERPILLARS

Tracy Nelson Maurer

A Crabtree Seedlings Book

CRABTREE
Publishing Company
www.crabtreebooks.com

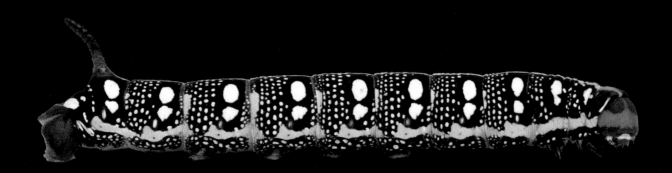

TABLE OF CONTENTS

AMAZING CRAWLERS

Like all insects, caterpillars have three body sections and six true legs. The other legs are called prolegs.

proleg
Prolegs are attached to the abdomen.

abdomen
The abdomen consists of ten segments.

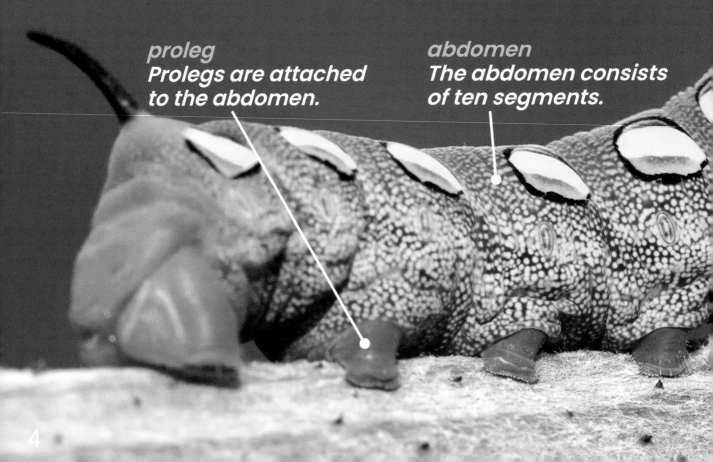

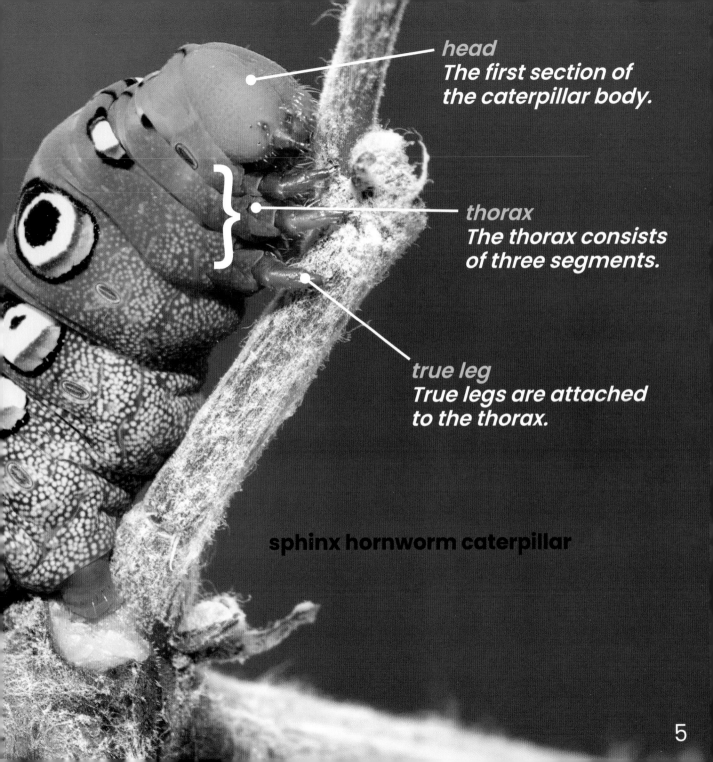

head
The first section of the caterpillar body.

thorax
The thorax consists of three segments.

true leg
True legs are attached to the thorax.

sphinx hornworm caterpillar

Caterpillars do not have lungs. They breathe through holes in their skin.

imperial moth caterpillar

Breathing holes line caterpillar bodies.

TRICKY LOOKS

Caterpillars can be tiny, huge, smooth, hairy, spiny, or covered in goo.

saturniid moth caterpillar

CREEPY OR COOL?

The harmless hickory horned devil moth caterpillar grows up to 6 inches (15 centimeters) long. It's one of the world's largest caterpillars.

Birds, mice, spiders, and other insects eat caterpillars. Caterpillars often use their looks to avoid becoming dinner.

Giant swallowtail butterfly caterpillars avoid becoming dinner by looking like bird poop!

False eyes on the spicebush swallowtail caterpillar frighten predators.

Many caterpillars use camouflage to hide from **predators**. Others use bright colors to warn predators to stay away.

Geometrid caterpillars look like part of a plant.

Monarch butterfly caterpillars are poisonous. Stripes mean, "stay away."

FIERCE EATERS

Caterpillars live to eat! Most caterpillars eat plants. Their strong, hard jaws cut like scissors.

mandibles
Jaws used for chewing.

CReePY OR COOL?

Some caterpillars are carnivores. They eat spiders, insects, or insect eggs.

LIFE CYCLE

Caterpillar eggs are laid on the caterpillars' favorite food plants. The eggs often look like tiny pearls or clumps of hard bubbles.

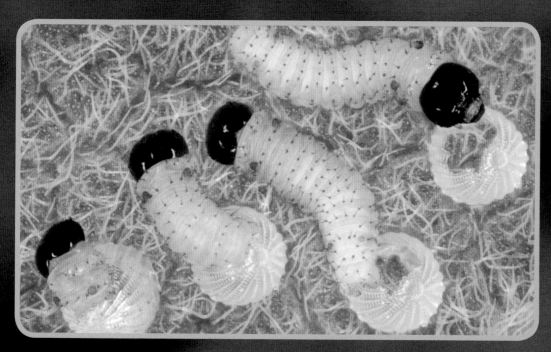

Monarch caterpillars hatch from their eggs and then eat the shells.

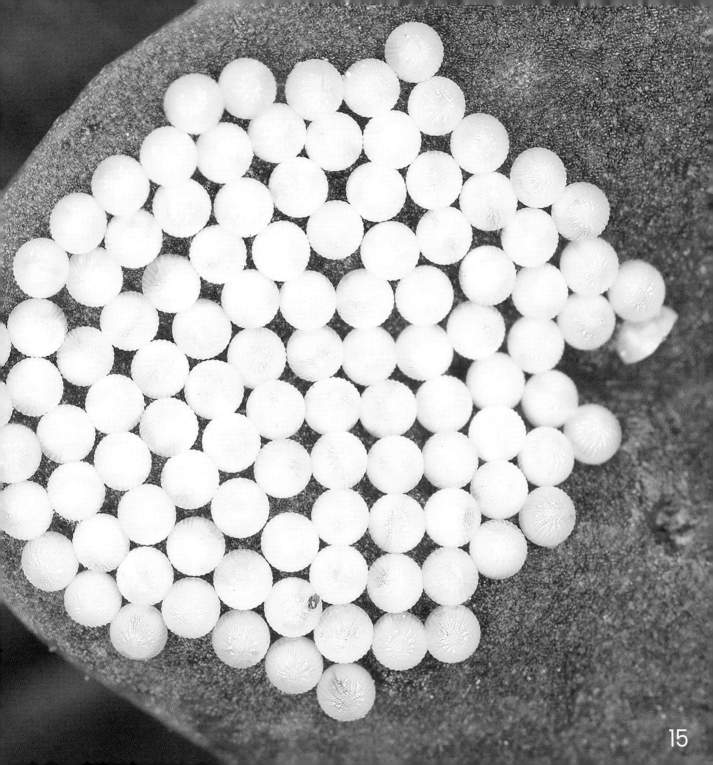

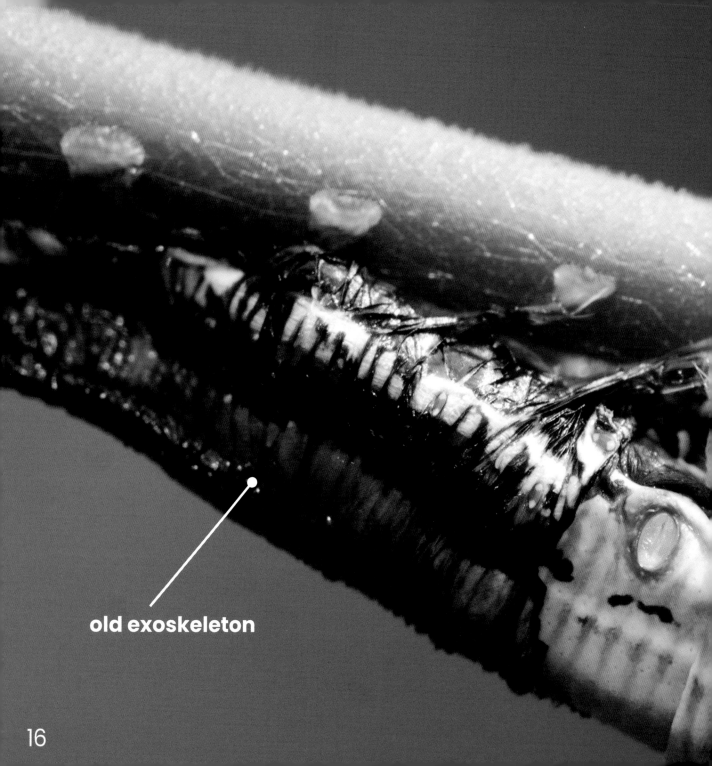

old exoskeleton

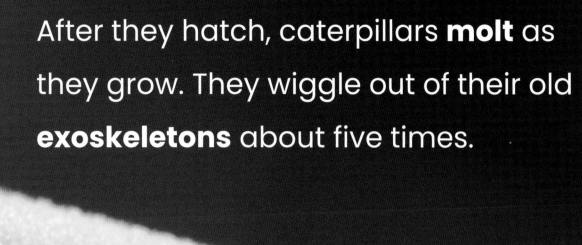

After they hatch, caterpillars **molt** as they grow. They wiggle out of their old **exoskeletons** about five times.

These monarch caterpillars are at the pupa stage of their life cycle.

At the pupa stage, butterfly caterpillars form a **chrysalis** and moth caterpillars spin a silk **cocoon**.

butterfly chrysalis

moth cocoon

Inside the chrysalis or cocoon,
the caterpillar's body changes.

It turns into a butterfly or moth. Amazing!

WHAT DID YOU LEARN?

Answer each question. Find a sentence in the book that proves your answer.

1. Caterpillars are insects because they
   a. have six true legs.
   b. have many body sections.
   c. come in many different colors.

2. Caterpillars hatch from eggs.
   True   False

3. Which sentence is not true?
   a. Caterpillars breathe through holes in their skin.
   b. Growing caterpillars molt one time.
   c. Many caterpillars use camouflage to hide from predators.

Answers: 1. a, 2. True, 3. b

GLOSSARY

chrysalis (KRISS-uh-liss): The special protective shell in which a butterfly pupa changes to an adult

cocoon (KAH-koon): The woven, protective covering in which moth caterpillars change to adults

exoskeletons (ex-oh-SKEL-uh-tunz): Hard, outer cases that support the body of animals without bones

molt (MOHLT): To shed skin or an outer covering, so the animal can grow

predators (PRED-uh-turz): Animals that hunt other animals for food

pupa (PYOO-puh): The stage of growth between caterpillar and adult that occurs in a hard shell

INDEX

School-to-Home Support for Caregivers and Teachers

This book helps children grow by letting them practice reading. Here are a few guiding questions to help the reader build his or her comprehension skills. Possible answers appear here in red.

Before Reading

- **What do I think this book is about?** *I think this book is about cool caterpillars. I think this book is about how caterpillars turn into butterflies.*

- **What do I want to learn about this topic?** *I want to learn how caterpillars move. I want to learn what caterpillars eat.*

During Reading

- **I wonder why...** *I wonder why caterpillars turn into butterflies. I wonder why some caterpillars are so pretty.*

- **What have I learned so far?** *I have learned that some caterpillars are carnivores that eat spiders, insects, and insect eggs. I have learned that most caterpillars eat plants.*

After Reading

- **What details did I learn about this topic?** *I have learned that caterpillars do not have lungs, they breathe through holes in their skin. I have learned that there are caterpillars that turn into butterflies and some that turn into moths.*

- **Read the book again and look for the glossary words.** *I see the word **pupa** on page 18, and the word **chrysalis** on page 19. The other glossary words are found on page 23.*

Library and Archives Canada Cataloguing in Publication

Title: Caterpillars / Tracy Nelson Maurer.
Names: Maurer, Tracy Nelson, 1965- author.
Description: Series statement: Creepy but cool | "A Crabtree seedlings book".
  | Includes index. | Previously published in electronic format by Blue Door
  Publishing FL in 2015.
Identifiers: Canadiana (print) 20210201886 |
  Canadiana (ebook) 20210201894 |
  ISBN 9781427161642 (hardcover) |
  ISBN 9781427161765 (softcover) |
  ISBN 9781427161888 (HTML) |
  ISBN 9781427162007 (EPUB) |
  ISBN 9781427162120 (read-along ebook)
Subjects: LCSH: Caterpillars—Juvenile literature.
Classification: LCC QL544.2 .M38 2022 | DDC j595.7813/92—dc23

Library of Congress Cataloging-in-Publication Data

Names: Maurer, Tracy Nelson, 1965- author.
Title: Caterpillars / Tracy Nelson Maurer.
Description: New York : Crabtree Publishing, [2022] | Series: Creepy but
  cool - a Crabtree seedlings book | Includes index.
Identifiers: LCCN 2021018423 (print) |
  LCCN 2021018424 (ebook) |
  ISBN 9781427161642 (hardcover) |
  ISBN 9781427161765 (paperback) |
  ISBN 9781427161888 (ebook) |
  ISBN 9781427162007 (epub) |
  ISBN 9781427162120
Subjects: LCSH: Caterpillars--Juvenile literature.
Classification: LCC QL544.2 .M287 2022 (print) | LCC QL544.2 (ebook) |
  DDC 595.7813/92--dc23
LC record available at https://lccn.loc.gov/2021018423
LC ebook record available at https://lccn.loc.gov/2021018424

Crabtree Publishing Company

www.crabtreebooks.com   1–800–387–7650

Print book version produced jointly with Blue Door Education in 2022

Written by Tracy Nelson Maurer
Print coordinator: Katherine Berti

Printed in the U.S.A./062021/CG20210401

Photo credits: www.shutterstock.com - www.istock.com. Cover © Alex_187 - Page 2-3 istock.com/GlobalP. page 4-5 © Palo_ok. page 6-7 © Matt Jeppson. Page 8-9 © Dr. Morley Read. page 9 creepy but cool callout © Matt Jeppson, page 10 top photo © Tyler Fox, bottom photo © Dean Evangelista. page 11 top photo © Tyler Fox, bottom © James Laurie. page 12, 13 © KratochvilP. page 14-15 © Henrik Larsson, inset photo © Cathy Keifer. page 16-17 © Johan Larson. page 18 © Cathy Keifer. page 19 top © PhotonCatcher, bottom © Eric. Isselee. page 20-21 © Laurie Barr

Published in the United States
Crabtree Publishing
347 Fifth Ave.
Suite 1402-145
New York, NY 10016

Published in Canada
Crabtree Publishing
616 Welland Ave.
St. Catharines, Ontario
L2M 5V6